DAUGHTER
LESSONS

By Bernadette Catalana

ISBN: 9798813090936

DEDICATION

Most people believe that I have raised my daughters. The opposite, in fact, is true. They have elevated me, have given me purpose, and most notably, have brought me great joy and happiness. So naturally, this book is dedicated to the precious girls who raised me, making my life better than I ever dreamed it could be.

ACKNOWLEDGEMENTS

A special thank you to Vickijo Campanaro, Craig Bullock, Katie Melia, Mary McFee, Julie Blue, and The Assisi Institute for their invaluable assistance in launching *Daughter Lessons*.

TABLE OF CONTENTS

INTRODUCTION

I began *Daughter Lessons* as a personal writing project several years ago. At the time, my daughters were growing up and gaining their independence, and I was trying to imagine life without seeing them every day. Then another thought came — a tougher one — that eventually they would be living life completely without me. Completely. Although I hoped that day was (and is) far away, I decided to plan for it. Each day for a month, I sat down and composed a lesson. I wrote about things they would want to know about life, about love, and about their mother. I began on October first and by Halloween, I had 31 lessons and over 18,000 words.

There began *Daughter Lessons*, a simple idea inspired by my daughters and fueled by my love for them. As time went on and I looked at those humble musings, I realized that many of the lessons applied beyond the bounds of our trio, so in December 2014 we launched the *Daughter Lessons* blog together. My original plan was to publish a weekly lesson, but life — as it often does — got in the way. That said, we have managed to keep posting. This collection contains a sampling, loosely falling into three categories: Lead (basic ingredients to lead a good life); Learn (what I've learned along the way); and Love (because that's all that really matters). This volume is not meant to be read from cover to cover, but in any order that makes sense or feels right to the reader. I claim no moral authority and fully acknowledge that everyone's experiences are unique to them. What emerges as universal are the challenges, triumphs, fears, and joys that flow from being one of many daughters of a single mother and a mother of daughters. Enjoy.

LEAD

TRUTH

"This above all: to thine own self be true."
- William Shakespeare in Hamlet

Be true to yourself. You have heard this phrase or variations of it many times, but have you ever stopped to think about what it really means? Being true to who you are is important for the simple fact that you are the one person you are going to be with, and be responsible to, your entire life. This is a truth you will come back to over and over again.

The first step in being true to yourself is knowing who you are. Who you are is made up of, among other things, what you like or don't like, what you believe or don't believe, what you can stand, withstand, understand, or can't stand, what you love, whom you love, and whom you can never love. Knowing who you are is a challenge that will not end. If in your heart you know what feels right for you at a particular moment, even if you might not be able to express it in words, go with that, especially when you are in doubt. Some situations require self-truth and direct advice:

- Don't date someone just because that someone likes or is infatuated with you; it is a recipe for disaster.
- Don't kiss someone because you feel sorry for them or for any reason other than you want to kiss them; the body doesn't lie.

- Don't wear any item of clothing that makes you uncomfortable, even for a short period of time; you will be tortured until you can take the regrettable item off.
- Don't take a job solely for the money or benefits; you will grow accustomed to the income but will be miserable each time you go to work.
- Don't miss the opportunity to fall in love. When you feel it, go with it, because you never know when you will have the chance again.

Finally, no matter how much someone loves you (your parents), no matter how much someone depends on you (your children), or no matter how much someone idolizes you (parents, children, and those who follow you on social media), accountability to yourself has to be first and foremost. If someone disagrees with you but truly cares for you, they will eventually come around. If they don't, the sooner you find out the better.

GRATITUDE

"Blessed be Thou for having sustained us until this day."
- Elie Wiesel, Nobel Prize Speech, 1986

We have so much to be grateful for. As I am sitting here writing this, I am awed and humbled by the blessings in my life — awed at the enormity of God's goodness and humbled because often I am not grateful. It can be easier to focus on what I don't have and what I didn't get, as opposed to realizing that I have exactly what I need.

The first time I read Elie Wiesel's Nobel Prize speech, I was struck by the simplicity and profundity of its beginning. First, he explained to his audience that in the Jewish tradition, one is duty-bound on any special occasion to begin with a prayer of gratitude, and then he went on to pray the short prayer you see above. Here was this man who had witnessed the horrors of Auschwitz and lost his childhood, his parents, his baby sister, his home, and the vast majority of his people, yet he was obligated to be grateful to the God who sustained him. What an eye-opener for me, who had not in my lifetime endured 1/100th of what this man endured by the time he was 16. At that moment, I felt guilty for ever complaining about my life.

It is only human to get down. Our inner eye jumps to what's wrong, but the next time you are feeling sorry for yourself, ask what's right. Put it down on paper and post it where you will easily see this reminder of what you have to be grateful for, what is right in your life, and how you have been sustained.

I have hit rock bottom more than once. At one particularly low point I had just started a new job after going through several major upheavals. I didn't think I could handle another change, but I had to make it work because there were no other options. After feeling sorry for myself for an extended period, I decided I had to pull it together. The first thing I did was make a list of five things for which I was most grateful. I stuck it to the front of my computer on a post-it note, so I had a constant reminder of the many blessings in my life. My five things were: 1. beautiful daughters; 2. improved job situation; 3. good friends; 4. health; and 5. magical house. My number one is constant, and although numbers 2-5 are subject to revision, I still use the post-it note of gratitude on the front of my computer as a tool to remind me of what's right in my life.

FAITH

"Faith consists in believing when it is beyond
the power of reason to believe."
- Voltaire

Much of what I know about faith I learned from my mother or Grammy, as she is lovingly known to many. One of my earliest memories of Grammy's strong faith dates back to a summer day in 1975. It was August 15 (the Feast of the Assumption) and Grammy, my sister Elaine, my brother Paul, and I were making the long walk home from mass. It was sweltering. We were on foot because we didn't have a car. That was probably just as well because no one in the house knew how to drive — that is, until my sister Ann got her license that summer. With one licensed driver in the family we could think about getting a car, which would help with the arduous task of getting the groceries for eight people home. Our current system involved multiple trips to the grocery store each day on foot.

Once Ann passed her road test, Grammy decided she was going to pray for a car. Oh, there were plenty of cars, but few we could afford to buy, and the only thing we actually could afford was free. So, Grammy started praying. She said the rosary each day for 60 days: the first 30 days in Petition (asking for what she wanted) and the second 30 days in Thanksgiving (being grateful for getting what she wanted, which assumed she was going to get it). Day 60 just happened to fall on August 15 and the weight of my mother's unanswered prayer was on us all as we trudged home from church. Although it was obvious Grammy was discouraged, she managed to say, as she often did, "Blessed Mother never fails me."

As we neared the house, we heard the phone ringing. Elaine and I ran up the steps and through the house to grab it before the caller hung up (this was pre-voicemail and pre-answering machine). It was Grammy's friend Loretta. And although we handed over the receiver we all stayed close enough to hear her say: "We found you a car!" I will never forget my mother's joy. That singular moment gave me my first real taste of miracles.

Another Grammy miracle is the Christmas Eve Miracle (yes, there had to be one). Grammy and her best friend, Lorraine Naro, volunteered to help Endicott's local bottle lady (a woman who supported herself by returning bottles and cans). She had been hit by a vehicle while she pushed her bottle-filled shopping cart across the street. After she was released from the hospital, they picked her up, cleaned her apartment which was packed to the rafters with bottles, and generally helped her get back on her feet. They even found a lawyer to file a lawsuit against the driver who hit her. A few months later on Christmas Eve, Grammy and Lorraine stopped to give the Bottle Lady a Christmas gift. She said she had a gift for them as well and handed each an envelope with $1,000 cash inside! The Bottle Lady then explained that she actually had quite a bit of money. She had been the executive assistant to the head of IBM for many years and never married or had children. Collecting bottles was merely a lifestyle choice. Grammy was so happy, not just at receiving the money, but because she gave without expectation of getting back and was rewarded generously for her efforts. Once again, the joyous look on my mother's face when she recounted the story on Christmas Day was the only evidence I needed that miracles are our birthright and a reward for keeping the faith.

HEROES

"As you get older it is harder to have heroes,
but it is sort of necessary."
- Ernest Hemingway

It is not only important to look for the good in people; it is also important to find things to admire and emulate. People who have exceptionally good character or who have overcome life's challenges with grace and dignity are prime candidates to serve as heroes and role models. I have several.

Mother Teresa

"Let us always meet each other with a smile, for the smile is the beginning of love."

Mother Teresa gave up a life of comfort and ease to care for the poor of India. A gentle person who led others by example, her life was about giving to and loving the lowly and the poor.

Elie Wiesel

"When a person doesn't have gratitude, something is missing in his or her humanity. A person can almost be defined by his or her attitude toward gratitude."

Elie Wiesel lost his family and home, emerging from Auschwitz to write one of the most powerful accounts of the Holocaust. Despite this devastation, he lived a life filled with thanksgiving.

Mahatma Gandhi

"Victory attained by violence is tantamount to a defeat, for it is momentary."

Gandhi was a lawyer turned political and spiritual activist. He fought for the rights of South Africans and then his own people, the people of India. He ultimately led a revolution against one of the most powerful countries on earth, Great Britain, and succeeded without violence.

Vincent Van Gogh

"I know for sure that I have an instinct for color, and that it will come to me more and more, that painting is in the very marrow of my bones."

It would be easy to dismiss Van Gogh, like many do, as an insane genius. Although he lived a tortured life, he stayed true to himself when it came to his art and never compromised the future for the immediate, as if he knew he was painting for the ages.

Coco Chanel

"Fashion is not something that exists in dresses only. Fashion is in the sky and in the street. Fashion has to do with ideas, the way we live, and what is happening."

Coco Chanel was a fashion trailblazer. Her cutting-edge sense of style literally transformed the way women dressed. Her life's work began in an orphanage where she learned how to sew.

The Dalai Lama

"Joy is the simplest form of gratitude."

In exile the Dalai Lama found freedom to do for his people what he could not do in his native Tibet. I have heard him speak multiple times and am always struck by his joyfulness.

Although I have named some famous heroes and heroines, you will find many people in your daily life to admire and emulate. My inner circle is filled with those that have outstanding qualities that I try to channel when I need exactly their particular superpower. The qualities I look for in others most are dignity, generosity, joyfulness, compassion, and most of all, kindness.

HAPPINESS

"There is no duty we so underrate
as the duty of being happy."
- Robert Louis Stevenson

This topic involves something that everyone is looking for, but few actually find. For many years I too have devoted myself to the pursuit of happiness, mostly by trying to change things that made me unhappy. Unfortunately, changing things can make you even more unhappy than when you started, but only for a while. Too many people stay in unhappy situations because it is comfortable for them; in effect, they are "comfortably uncomfortable," but they remain because they would rather stick with what they know than venture out into the world and take a chance on something more. Yet sometimes you have to take the whole house down in order to rebuild it exactly the way you want.

Don't be afraid of going after what you want because no one else is going to do it for you. Be fierce in the pursuit of your own happiness—even if it gets messy for a while. Ultimately, the dust will clear. From the outside looking in, my life looked pretty messy for a while: death, divorce, job changes, address changes, children growing up and moving on. I am sure that many were certain that my life was "trending down." But I can assure you, although the picture from above may not have always looked so rosy, I knew I was on the right path because inside I felt solid.

That period of transition allowed me to find out who I am, who I am not, and what I wanted and didn't want. In this way I built my version of an authentic life.

Probably the best thing I have realized while searching for happiness is that it can be found in both reaching the goal (getting a new job, finding the one, buying the dream house) and in all the wonderful moments that happen while moving toward the goal. For example, buying the oldest house in Rochester and fixing it up was a wonderful goal. When I reached the moment where the old falling down house was actually a beautiful home because of my care, I was so happy. But I also had countless happy moments along the way each and every day. For the first full year, I woke up nearly every morning and looked around the former ballroom-turned-bedroom and whispered to myself: "I can't believe this is my house!" Happiness is two things: reaching high for whatever it is you want but also remembering to look close at what it is you have and enjoying it in the moment, exactly as it is. If you can master the art of doing those two things simultaneously, you will live a happy life.

PRAYER

"Prayer is better than sleep."
- Saad

I am writing this in the meditation room of 70 East Boulevard because I am not quite sure what I am going to write. These days, I am praying so much, it is effortless. It is constant. It is like breathing; I never have to think about it. I pray throughout the day wherever I am, but I start and end each day here in this room. That practice centers me and brings me peace, and if I miss that dedicated time, I don't feel complete.

My role models for prayer are my mother (no surprise) and my father's mother, Grandma Weaver. Grammy is famous for her praying. I admit, I used to roll my eyes at her and think that praying was all she ever did. Sometimes I wonder if my daughters say such things about me, but I quickly wipe that thought from my mind — worse things could be said! In that one way, I am like my mother.

My Grandma Weaver was my favorite person in the whole world until I had my children. She was gentle, sweet and "holy," in the good way. You could feel her kindness. But when it came to prayer, she was a warrior! I have never seen anyone, not even Grammy, pray with such focus. To please God, she

16

had a practice of "giving things up" as an offering along with her prayers in the hopes of getting her intention. For example, when one of her many babies had pneumonia, often a deadly illness in the days before antibiotics, my Grandma Weaver prayed for his recovery and offered to give up sweets FOR THE REST OF HER LIFE if he got better! And because he lived, she did. She made other such deals with God as well, and from what I heard, all were successful: she got what she was praying for. It appeared that the sacrifices added some mojo to her prayers. As an adult, I sometimes wonder if her prayers would have been answered in the same manner if she hadn't vowed never to eat meat on Thursdays or watch television on Fridays. I guess it doesn't matter because doing the extra offering made her feel more in control of situations where, in fact, she had none.

To me, prayer is not about control; it is the opposite. It is about surrendering to something that is bigger than we are, yet part of us. Jesus told us, "The kingdom of heaven is within (Luke 17:20-21)." So, it makes sense that when we pray, we look to what is inside for strength, answers, comfort, and peace. Sometimes I just sit trying not to think of anything, letting thoughts come and go without latching onto them. You don't need words; nor do you have to be sitting or kneeling. Just going about your day can be done in a way that is an offering. Sometimes it helps to have a mantra to keep you calm and focused. I have gone through many and am always changing them. The one I have been saying most often lately is simply, "Thank you."

HOPE

"The wings of hope carry us, soaring
high above the driving winds of life."
-Ana Jacob

I have two simple stories of hope. Both are about my friend Vicki's son Evan, who severed his spinal cord in an accident while he was making a snow angel for his younger sisters. He has been a quadriplegic since 1997. As you can imagine, hope was not plentiful at that time, but it was very much needed. Often hope comes in the form of laughter. Being able to find something to laugh about when times are bleak can bring sweet diversion and comfort.

The days after Evan's injury were dark. I was so worried for Evan and for my dear friend Vicki. Probably the most frustrating part was not being able to see or talk to her, as she was consumed with Evan's care. When we finally spoke on the phone almost two weeks later, it was such a relief to hear her voice. After we addressed the obvious topic, I tried to make small talk in a weak attempt to be normal. I commented that until recently I had never known her full name was Vicki-Jo. Then, without thinking, I blurted out that maybe she should change her name to "Vicki-Job" after the

Biblical figure whose faith was tested through a series of tragedies. As lame as that joke was, we both started authentically laughing. It made me feel better and yes, hopeful, when I heard her sweet laughter on the other end of the line.

Another way that hope stays alive is through the little signs we get at what always seems to be exactly the right time, often our lowest point. A sign of hope came my way about a month after Evan's accident, literally in the form of an angel. A fundraising group was started to defray the enormous medical and home renovation expenses that were not covered by insurance. Due to the circumstances of his injury, we called ourselves "Evan's Angels." There were several stories in the paper about Evan and the group's fundraising efforts. One day, Vicki called to let me know that she had identified me to a newspaper reporter as the person responsible for handling any donations. Inside I panicked, but I calmly told her that it was no problem. As I hung up the phone, I was filled with fear; I had two small children and had started my career as a lawyer not even a year before. Where would I find the time?

The very next day we received our first donation. It was from a woman traveling through Rochester on business who read Evan's story in the local paper. She had tucked a check for a thousand dollars inside a card with the most beautiful angel on the front. When I saw the angel, tears flowed from my tired eyes. That sign was meant just for me, to let me know that I would have everything I needed to help my friend. That angel meant so much to me that I later bought a large reproduction of the print for myself, Debbie, our Evan's Angels leader, and of course, Vicki. Every time I look at the angel, I am reminded of that sign of hope and how it inspired me to believe in myself and what I could do when put to the test. Over the course of ten years, people donated more than half a million dollars for Evan's care. I managed every penny and wrote every check on his behalf. That little sign of hope carried me a long way and helped me carry my friend and her son when they were in need.

COURAGE

"Fire is the test of gold; adversity,
of strong (wo)men."
- Seneca

I have avoided disclosing that I am not really all that crazy about
my name. Bernadette is long, old-fashioned, and cumbersome,
not to mention the fact that everyone wants to shorten it and call
me Bern or Bernie, which I hate. What I do like, though, is the
meaning attached to my name. By all accounts, Bernadette
means "brave as a bear." Yet despite my name, I often felt racked
with fear.

As a child, I was terrified of the dark, dogs, and even men —
especially men. Unfortunately, we had both a large man and a
large dog, Pickles, living next door. I was terrified of both.
Anytime the man so much as looked at me, I ran away crying. I
had the exact same reaction to Pickles and any other dog that
crossed my path: a primal response of terror. Unfortunately for
the woman next door, but fortunately for me, the man eventually
moved out. I am not sure what happened to Pickles.

No, I am decidedly not brave in the traditional sense. My brand
of bravery is different. I am brave with words. I am brave with
feelings. Often, I am brave in putting feelings into words and

articulating things that others might feel but wouldn't dare say. I am also brave because I am willing to acknowledge that I am scared, but I continue on just the same.

Here are some of the bravest things I have done in my life:

- I told my fourth-grade teacher, Mrs. Mancini, that I was not in the appropriate reading group. I told her that I should not be in the Blue Birds but was rightly a member of the Eagles. She told my Dad that I was so convincing that she immediately had me re-tested and promoted me. I completed all reading levels through the eighth grade by the end of fifth grade.

- I would not let my father give me away at my wedding; I thought it was hypocritical since he had missed much of my life. My mother did not want to embarrass my dad by taking the assignment. With that, I decided I would walk myself down the aisle. My father was not happy and neither was my mother-in-law, but I was immovable and walked down the aisle alone because that felt right to me.

- On the day my father died, after I had not slept or eaten for days, against the advice of my realtor and friend, I negotiated the deal for the Oliver Culver House, the oldest house in Rochester. I was honest and told the other side that though I had no money and was not in a position to close for another 9 months, I wanted to move in immediately. To indicate what I was willing to pay, I wrote what I thought was a fair price on a small piece of paper, almost $100,000 under the list price. I could see everyone at the table squirming, but surprisingly, the offer was accepted on the spot. As we walked out, my agent threw his arms around me, declaring me "brilliant." I didn't feel brilliant, but I did feel brave.

PRIDE

"A person may be proud without being vain.
Pride relates more to our opinion of ourselves;
vanity, to what we would have others think of us."
- Jane Austen, Pride and Prejudice

Pride is important but often hard to muster. Life can have a way of beating us down and tempting us to beat ourselves up. When I am feeling down on myself, it helps to think of the things in my life that make me proud. It can be a big thing, like graduating from law school, or it can be a small thing, like the fact that I make good sauce. I focus on all the good things, big and small, and try to forget the things that haven't gone so well. I read somewhere that true champions focus only on their strengths and don't spend that much time trying to fix their weaknesses. These things make me proud:

- I can throw a party and have as much fun as my guests.
- I can do a headstand and sometimes a handstand.
- I am known for my good taste.
- I am a hard worker.
- I have many friends, which leads me to believe that I am a good friend.

- I graduated from law school with honors even though I had two small children (maybe because I had two small children).
- I rehabilitated and revived the oldest house in Rochester.
- I have two beautiful daughters who are as kind as they are lovely.

Ask yourself regularly, what makes you proud to be you?

SPIRITUALITY

"All I have seen teaches me to trust
the Creator for all I have not seen."
- Ralph Waldo Emerson

Much of what defines your personal faith — your spirituality — is learned without a textbook. Your spiritual journey is completely and utterly unique. True spirituality is not formulaic; going to church + giving to charity + never swearing ≠ eternal life. Many people want a recipe to follow, a checklist which will ensure them that they will make it to heaven if only they do exactly the right things. Spirituality is about finding your own path home and owning your personal divinity. So, when it dawned on me that I might not necessarily be behind every single word of the traditional Catholic prayers I learned as a child, I decided to make my own prayers. The Apostles' Creed, for example, was testing my veracity. So, I went for the rewrite. Here is my own personal creed:

I believe in God, the father and the mother, the mightiest of mighty and the gentlest of all, and the maker and keeper of the universe. I believe Jesus was God-realized, a son of God. And I am God's daughter. I believe both of us were conceived to walk in goodness on the earth.

26

Though our bodies return to dust, our essence cannot be destroyed. I believe that hell is created when man acts as if we are separate from one another. I believe that Jesus defeated death, but I do not believe he will judge us harshly when we die — he above anyone realizes we are doing the best we can with what we know right now. I believe in the Holy Spirit and the quiet guidance I receive when I seek help. I believe that religion can be a guide on the road to the kingdom, but no single religion can claim supremacy. I believe in angels and in saints, sages, and gurus that have gone before me and stand beside me, giving heavenly support and strength. I believe we are one in our humanity. I believe in life. But mostly I believe in love and in its power to heal us and save us. Awomen. Amen.

DREAMS

"Reach high, for stars lie hidden in your soul.
Dream deep, for every dream precedes the goal."
-Pamela Vaull Starr

When I was young, I didn't have lofty ambitions. I didn't dream of going to law school. I became a lawyer so I could earn enough money to support my children and put my writing skills to good use. At one point I thought I wanted to be a hairdresser but was dissuaded by my older sisters. My one true dream, always, was to be a mother. No one could have talked me out of that, and that has worked out just fine because my children have taught me a lot about dreaming.

From the time she was in seventh grade, Carly knew she wanted to go to college in New York City. Despite the anxiety of certain family members, she made it happen. I was cleaning out her desk a few weeks after she left for Pace University and came across one of her junior high notebooks. On the back she wrote her five-year plan:

1. Get braces off; 2. make my parents proud of me for something; and 3. College - NYC. I immediately mailed the notebook to her with a note, letting her know she could cross every item off her list, especially #2!

From the moment Courtney tried on her first pink tutu at age two, she had a passion for ballet. Once she was on that path, there was no stopping her. Sure, she had doubts and she got discouraged, but she never gave up! It has been nothing short of magical to see her realize her highest hopes: dancing professionally.

Watching my girls pursue their dreams has inspired me to have some for myself. *Daughter Lessons* is just one of them. Dream on, beautiful dreamers!

YOGA

"Yoga is not about touching your toes;
it is what you learn on the way down."
- Jigar Gor

I have been practicing yoga for almost twenty years. When I found yoga, or more accurately, when yoga found me, I was a mess. I was working far too many hours and driving hundreds of miles each week between depositions, court appearances, and transporting my girls to and from school, activities, and home. In addition to those demands, I felt the added pressure most women feel to strive for physical perfection. My life was exhausting, yet no matter how tired I was, I could not shut off my mind. Constantly thinking about the next thing I had to do, I tried to be a step ahead but always felt a step behind. I was hurtling through time and space, arriving at destinations but having no idea how I got there. Rarely was I living in the moment.

One day, as I flew through yet another tour of duty, I noticed a new yoga studio. I knew little about yoga other than it was supposed to be a good workout. I decided on the spot to sign up for a class, and that single action changed everything. Seventy-five minutes flew by as I put all my concentration on learning the difficult poses. Not once did I think about anything other than the unfamiliar movements and my breathing. By the time class was over, I realized that by stepping onto my mat, I could step out of my life and recharge.

Yoga eventually became more than a temporary refuge as the mindfulness I learned in class carried over to the rest of my days. This newfound ability became essential during the following years, which challenged me with multiple losses. Because of the physical and spiritual strength I developed through yoga, weighty circumstances did not crush me; instead, I survived and thrived. I don't think I can quite make the claim that yoga saved my life as many current articles do, but I can say that yoga has made my life lighter, richer, calmer, more fluid, more real, and simply, better.

THE SECRET(S)

"The longer I live the more beautiful life becomes."
-Frank Lloyd Wright

My blog sister Amy and I have explored the quest for the key to life, more specifically, the key to a happy life. I have had much time to ponder the subject and conclude there is more than one secret! No single set applies to every person, so you must make up your own.

My top five:

- Life is short. To avoid regret, dream dreams, set goals, and make things happen.
- Value your own opinion above all others. If you are too concerned about what others say or think, they own you.
- You are stronger than you know. Even if the worst thing you can imagine happens, all will be well in the end.
- Attitude, not circumstances, determines your level of happiness.
- Love yourself first — all other loves flow from there.

LEARN

READ

"A book is like a garden carried in the pocket."
-Chinese Proverb

I always dreamed of living in a house with a library. And while I can check that wish off my bucket list, it really wasn't the space that enamored me; what filled the space was the true object of my adoration and a lifelong love: books. From a young age, I was rarely seen without a book in my hands. It did not matter what was going on around me; all I could see were the words on the page and a picture in my mind of what was unfolding.

Ironically, I started reading out of fear — not fear of bad grades, but fear of the dark. I was convinced there was a horrible fate waiting for me in the darkened hallway leading up to the third floor of our house on South Street. Eventually, my parents let me sleep with the hall light on, but the light was not enough. It made things worse because then I could see whatever grotesque creature was coming to get me. I was like a night watchman constantly on guard, and that blaring light kept me awake! One night, I decided that since it was so bright, I would read, and I found that diving into a book distracted me enough to escape.

From then on, I read every night until I fell asleep. Not surprisingly, I became a voracious reader. I read the entire

Bobbsey Twins series, then moved onto Nancy Drew, Trixie Belden, Encyclopedia Brown, the Hardy Boys, Chronicles of Narnia, Pippi Longstocking, and all the Mary Poppins books. The best day in school was Scholastic Book day for two reasons: first, you got the books you ordered a couple of weeks before; second, you got the listing and order form for the new books! I would read every book summary and carefully select my next books, which were usually 35 cents each. My standard order was 3 books for $1.05. Although we didn't have money to spare, my mother always let me order books. My favorite childhood book, *The Best Loved Doll* by Rebecca Caudill, remains a faithful companion. Just a glimpse of its sweet pink cover brings me back to the first time I held it.

I have forgotten many of the books I read in those early years, but what I read didn't matter; it was the act of reading that made all the difference. In the short run, reading brought me relief from a fear that was overtaking me. In the long run, it helped me become an excellent student and nourished a love of learning that has never diminished. A debilitating fear became the path to what has been one of the biggest influences on my life — sounds like the plot of a page turner!

SINK OR SWIM

"We've greatly exaggerated the risk of sinking,
without celebrating the value of swimming."
- Seth Godin

Although most people would look at me and think of me as successful, the truth is that I have failed at many things in my life. It has been a good thing that I never let failing at something stop me from trying again.

I remember my first real taste of failure as clearly as if it happened to me today and not many decades ago. When I was in first grade my mother made me take Red Cross swimming lessons at the local Boys and Girls Club. The beginners' level had three parts. The first part was taught by my older sister's friend, Betty. She was perky with a long ponytail and very sweet. Our classes consisted of learning to put our heads in the water, blowing bubbles, and holding onto a kick board and kicking like mad from one side of the pool to the other. I passed the first part of the beginners' level, no problem.

Part two was a different story. For the first time in my life, I had a male teacher. I cannot recall his name, but he was tall, blonde, and hairy. I was afraid of him, and it shut me down so much that I couldn't learn anything. I knew I wasn't doing well and was more afraid of the water every day, instead of less. Probably the worst moment of my life to that point came on the last day of class. We were supposed to get our progress reports mailed to us. I was so relieved because I knew I was not likely to pass but took comfort in the fact that I would find out in private. The big scary, hairy man (who was probably all of 18) gave us some final words of instruction and told us that we were a good class. Then he said, "In fact, all of you passed, except for you." As he said this, he pointed at me sitting on the edge of the group, shivering in my wet yellow bathing suit.

I was devastated. I had to go home and tell my mother. All my older, athletic sisters who never failed at anything would find out too. It was awful. I went home and sprawled out on the couch in our family room, distraught. Before too long, I turned on the television and, believe it or not, came across a movie about a crippled girl who secretly taught herself to swim and eventually became a champion swimmer. It was called *Million Dollar Mermaid* and starred Esther Williams. I was so inspired that I asked to repeat the swimming class the next day! I went on to pass beginners' level 2, and each swim class I took thereafter. I don't think I would have been so proud of those successes if I hadn't first suffered such a colossal failure.

Don't be afraid to fail. It is part of life, part of the process, and it can lead to even greater success than if you tried and immediately achieved your goal. Sometimes failing once can be all the incentive you need to go after something better, stronger, and harder than before. Remember, there is no real failure except the failure to try.

WORDS MEAN SOMETHING

"Whatever words we utter should be chosen with care, for people will hear them and be influenced by them for good or ill."
- Buddha

This is a hard lesson to learn and even harder to put into practice. So often talk is cheap. But the opposite concept should be your guide: words mean something. We build our lives with our actions, yes, but also with our words. Ask yourself: What do my words say about me? What story do they tell? Am I proud of that story?

Don't swear. Too many people swear. This is one of my pet peeves although I even use swear words sometimes, but not often. I have tried hard to avoid swearing because my father's frequent swearing scared me. I remember as a little girl hiding behind the couch because he would be swearing so loudly and angrily. When I became an adult, I would hear people swearing and think of my dad — which I am sure is something he did not particularly want to be remembered for. Swearing does not reflect intelligence (it gives the opposite impression) and is downright verbal violence. I will admit, there are times when only a curse word fits the particular situation with which you are confronted, such as when the computer crashes and you realize you haven't saved anything in the last five pages, or when you drive the car through the closed garage door! Certainly, in those isolated instances, you have my permission to swear AT THE TOP OF YOUR LUNGS! Otherwise, avoid it as much as possible.

When you are angry, don't say things that you will later regret. Some people use their anger as an excuse to say whatever pops into their heads and then use the excuse of being angry to later justify what they said. I was just mad; I didn't mean it. But I think anger can be like wine. The phrase *in vino veritas* means in wine there is truth. Wine lowers inhibitions, and we often find words and feelings coming out when we have had a little. I think anger works much the same way, making words fall out of our mouths that we would otherwise keep to ourselves. If that isn't bad enough, the recipient of the diatribe knows only too well that maybe you didn't mean to say what you said, but you actually meant what you said. We all know people who use angry words to bully, intimidate, feel superior, or let off steam. Don't be one of them. Once those words come out, you cannot pull them back in or erase them from the ears of the person to whom they were directed.

Keep your word. If you ask someone to get together — call them. If you tell someone you will volunteer for their fundraiser — show up. If you say you are going to a party — get there. Don't be the person that says one thing and does another. If you say you'll do something, think of the Nike slogan and just do it! You will be happy you did. The opposite also holds true: if you don't want to do something that someone has asked you to do, say no. No excuses, no apologies, just "no thank you."

In summary: say what you mean, mean what you say but don't let what you say be mean!

"WARRIOR"

Don't be fooled by how I walk.
Ignore the lilt when I talk.
I am a warrior.
Pay no mind to what I wear
Or the color of my hair;
I am powered within.
Just because I wear a skirt
And I might just flirt
Doesn't mean you'll beat me.
Though I might sigh, (I've been known to cry)
I never give up.
I don't look tough
But I like it rough.
You're courting trouble.
Forget the glasses and the sexy curl
I'm not just a girl; I am a warrior.

I almost forgot I wrote this poem until the day I was visiting colleagues across the hall and spied the book in which it was published sitting on Linda's desk. Maria bought it for her at a garage sale and they were enjoying the collection of poems and photos submitted by women from all over the world. I recounted for them what prompted me to write "Warrior."

40

I was getting ready for a trial. My opponent was a law school classmate with whom I had multiple cases. He took everything personally, including any little victory I earned for my clients. One evening, he called after office hours and was obviously surprised when I picked up the phone. Never one to miss the opportunity for a dig, he launched in: "Oh, I didn't expect to get you. Shouldn't you be home taking care of your children?" As someone who took her motherhood very seriously, his sexist remark stung me. But I was not quick enough and missed the opportunity to call him on it. When I hung up, my frustration and anger flowed directly onto the page as "Warrior."

Later that week, I spotted a call for poetry submissions posted in a local coffee shop, and I submitted my little poem. It was ultimately chosen for publication in *Susan B. & Me, an International Collection of Personal Writings and Photographs*. What an experience for me and one I would never have had but for the thoughtless words of another. Now I am grateful to my opponent, who inspired and reminded me that I am a warrior!

AFTER THE FALL

"Failure is not fatal; it is the courage
to continue that counts."
-Winston Churchill

After running and cross-training diligently for an entire winter, I looked forward to the warm weather like I never had before. I felt fit and strong and invincible. And in a split second, I was none of those things. Kelly and I were flying through the last part of a run. Inspired by longer days and better weather, we picked up the pace beyond my usual leisurely trot. I was pumped, so pumped that I failed to see a huge recess in the sidewalk which caught my foot and literally sent me flying. I landed squarely on my right shoulder. The loud snap that punctuated the spring air was my collarbone cracking in two.

Just like that game Chutes and Ladders, my climb to the height of fitness took a great deal of effort; the slide was instantaneous and humbling. But in hindsight, I do not regret what I now call The Fall. The fall taught me about the wonders of the human body, the power of the human spirit, and the outrageous cost of healthcare (even when you have insurance). The lessons I learned, in no particular order:

- When your collarbone is broken, you cannot move the associated arm, which is very inconvenient.
- Angels are everywhere; from a seemingly deserted street people appeared to help.
- Don't go to the emergency room for a broken bone if you can help it. You are better off in urgent care; it will cost less and you will be seen sooner.
- If you do go to the emergency room, on a Friday night no less, bring a friend who will make you laugh even though you are racked with pain. Kelly was that friend. She even stayed overnight after I was released.
- An injury requires rest to aid your recovery. Do as I say, not as I do!
- The body heals quickly. I ran after 4 weeks, did cross fit after 12 weeks, and yoga after 4 months.
- If your doctor, who has never seen you before and will never see you again, says you will not "be the same" following your injury, ignore him! Only you and your attitude can limit you.
- I am not invincible, but I am strong.
- The most important thing after a fall? Get up again.

DEAR MEAN GIRLS

"I have learned silence from the talkative, tolerance from the intolerant, and kindness from the unkind."
-Khalil Gibran

Dear Mean Girls from my past, you know who you are. I am writing to let you know that I forgive you. It is not your fault you were brought up in a home that allowed you to think you were the center of the universe and fostered a sense that you were the queen of all that. You learned to slap down anyone who appeared to be weak, challenged your supremacy, or both at the same time. You have probably not given a second thought to me since we last laid eyes on each other. But I have certainly thought about you... YOU are the number one reason I taught my children to be kind. And though I won't ever forget all that's gone down, I am willing to let it go because you helped me tackle one of the biggest challenges of motherhood. Thank you for the inspiration, bioches.

COUNTING SLEEP

"I have promises to keep and
miles to go before I sleep."
-Robert Frost

This is going to be a do as I say NOT do as I do lesson. I generally like to lead by example, but I am not a great person to follow when it comes to sleeping. Your role models for this lesson should be Grandpop Catalana and Peanut (if we only could have carried Grandpop around the way we carried Peanut). Sleep when you can and get as much as you need, regardless of whom you may offend in the process. Seriously, sleeping is one of the kindest things you can do for yourself and your family! I say this as someone who has rarely, in my adult life, felt truly rested. Ironically, the night before two of the biggest days in my life, I did not sleep at all. Luckily, on both occasions, everything worked out all right, but I sure wish I could have a do over on both, as I would have liked to enjoy them or have been more aware of them.

Wedding (1988) The evening of June 10th was the usual night before a wedding. We had the rehearsal dinner at a local restaurant. However, given the crazy make-up of your dad's family and mine, nothing was typical. There was tension coming from your dad's camp because several of the in-laws, including your Grandmom, felt that we were getting married "out of order." Apparently, marriage order had to match birth order in your dad's family. We never got that memo and we decided to get married, even though Uncle Frank was still a bachelor. Because of this faux pas, we were being punished with a great many evil eyes, which upset me. As for my family, it was the usual free for all over at Grammy's house and somehow there was no place for me to sleep, even though I was the bride! Can you imagine, I had to sleep on the couch the night before my wedding. Add on to this that Aunt Ann and Uncle Steve decided they were going to go out and leave baby Zachary behind. I loved Zach, but he could hardly be described as a good sleeper. I did not sleep a single wink the night before I got married.

Bar exam (1995) The two of you were with your Grandmom in New Jersey for two weeks while I studied and took the exam. Courtney would cry every time we talked on the phone. I had never slept in a hotel room by myself. I was so nervous about taking the exam, failing the exam, and having to take the exam over if I failed, which meant being separated from the two of you, again. All those factors contributed to the stew of sleeplessness that plagued me that night. To make matters worse, I had only slept about three hours the night before, for the same reasons. I arrived at the test in a distraught state but managed to pull myself together. The first day of the exam was relatively smooth. I got by on sheer adrenalin. I tried to sleep at my friend Lori's house the night between day one and day two and I did, all of about four hours (the adrenalin kept me awake). I sailed through the morning of the Multi-State Bar Exam and then fell asleep in the afternoon session. I woke with 30 minutes left and 30 questions left to answer! It is a true miracle I finished and passed.

SOME THINGS YOU NEVER OUTGROW

"No one heals himself by wounding another."
- St. Ambrose

I have been the target of bullies my entire life. You would think that by now I would know how to avoid, or better yet, defeat my tormentors. But alas, the only thing that has changed is the identity of the person or persons that have me in their viewfinder. It is embarrassing that a woman at my age and stage and station can be subject to such humiliation. But for that very reason, I want to share my experience and somehow "write" my way to a solution. Before I started composing, I did some research on bullies. I was surprised to find that bullying, even in the workplace, is quite common. Upon reflection, this makes sense. The ability to bully is based on power differentials and the workplace is filled with those. My research also got me thinking about ghosts of bullies past. In 1st and 2nd grade there was B_D_, whom my mother mistakenly thought was a friend and therefore agreed to sleepovers, play dates and countless other activities on my behalf. After her, there were the "sporty" girls from Saint Anthony's who were responsible for my perpetual hatred of Phys. Ed. In high school, there was the big-busted prom queen a grade ahead. She hated me because her boyfriend was putting unrequested poems in my locker. She did not possess a poet's heart herself and made my life miserable until she graduated. I have had revenge, somewhat, although I doubt she knows. During one particularly painful bus ride, she overheard me saying that I might like to be a lawyer. Although she was not actually in the conversation, she loudly condemned the idea, and me, for having the gall to dream that big. I have thought of her with some satisfaction, having proved her prophecy wrong. No less hurtful than the tyrants of childhood were the bullies I encountered at work. Some of the abuse came at the hands of female law partners who repeatedly had lunch in plain sight, never asking me to join, while accusing me of many things, including undermining the partnership by "fraternizing" with the secretaries. Relief came only when I changed firms. But sometimes bullies are unavoidable. I have not only struggled to free myself of bullies, but to determine what is wrong with me or, more constructively, what is the universe trying to teach me by bringing me back to this storyline, again and again. I don't have that answer. I can tell you this: even considering my history, I would rather be the target than the bully. A bully can never escape from herself.

CHOICES

"I choose...to live by choice, not by
chance.
To make changes, not excuses.
To be motivated, not
manipulated. To be useful,
not used. To excel, not
compete. I choose
self-esteem, not self-pity.
I choose to listen to my inner voice. Not
the random opinion of others."
- Unknown

One of the things that we often take for granted are the choices that we have. Often we assume we are stuck in certain situations with no way out and no options. That is rarely true. In virtually every situation, there is a choice to accept the status quo or make a move to change what you don't like, don't want, or cannot or should not accept. So, don't fall into the trap of feeling helpless; know that you have choices every single day, even if it is only the choice to adjust your attitude about what is happening. Remember, your thoughts shape your life — so be careful what you think.

And when the dust finally settles after the turmoil, the real work begins. The challenge increases because the choices are not clear cut. Although stay v. move; new job v. same job; stay together v. move apart, etc. are all life-altering decisions, they are fairly well-defined. What is really hard is trying to find your footing after shaking up your life in an effort to live honestly. How do you relieve loneliness, find peace, continue to grow, build a life around yourself, by yourself? The answers to those questions are much more subtle than a simple yes or no, stay or go. The question becomes: Now what?

During my first forty-day yoga challenge, I wrote what has become known as my 40 Day Manifesto. I wrote it on the 40th day of the program and brought it to class to share with my group. It did not take long to write and is definitely not the most eloquent expression of thought. I was floored to learn, afterwards, how many people were moved by this declaration of intention. Several women who were in the program reached out to say that my words resonated with them and inspired them to take up the challenge—to live, not just survive, and to stop deferring their happiness until after they reach a certain goal or level of recognition.

My 40 Day Manifesto: This is going to be the best year of my life. I am going to make the same commitment to that goal as I made to the 40 Day Yoga Program and be just as diligent in "showing up" to pursue my quest for happiness and joy. The time is NOW. No more waiting to start my life after: I make peace with my birth family; find the right guy; get my house exactly the way I want it; or (you fill in the blank). I am not waiting for anyone or anything. There is no better, more perfect time to start than today. I am on my way to the best year of my life. Won't you join me?

Don't wait for some arbitrary someday to be happy. Make this the best year of your lives. That magical someday may never arrive.

RUN LIKE A GIRL

"Give a girl the right shoes and
she can conquer the world."
-Marilyn Monroe

Today my sister Margaret is running her twelfth "Boston," 40 years after her first. Because of her and all the other women who literally ran ahead to blaze the trail, it is hard to fathom a time when women were denied access. I cried upon seeing the 1967 photos of Kathrine Switzer being accosted by Boston Marathon officials when they discovered her running what had been to that time a men's race. Last year marked the 50th anniversary of Switzer's breakthrough, and she was interviewed by numerous media outlets. Her wisdom that resonated with me most was, "We've come a light year but still have a long way to go." Yes ladies, on many fronts, we need to keep running like THAT girl!

TO MY YOUNGER SISTERS ON GETTING OLDER

"Wrinkles should merely indicate
where the smiles have been."
- Mark Twain

Dear little sisters:

I have been a refuge for more than a few of you when you face big birthdays, or that first gray hair, or the last child leaving home. People seek my advice because I am a veteran of many milestones associated with the passage of time. I often laugh at the incredulity shown when others learn my age, or even better, the ages of my children. But I admit, for most, age is a serious matter. I have been interrogated about my skincare rituals and facial treatments, diet protocols and exercise routines. My medicine cabinet has been subjected to thorough inspection. I will not lie and say those things don't matter. They do, because they help to keep the outside reflective of the inside, the part of us immune to erosion. Indeed, the inside and the outside are connected. Pretty thoughts can prompt a pretty smile, highlighting your face better than any selfie light. Most importantly, keep in mind that age is a privilege NOT extended to everyone. Wear it with pride and a fabulous pair of shoes, knowing that you are in great company.

A ROSE BY ANY OTHER NAME

"That which we call a rose by any
other name would smell as sweet."
-William Shakespeare

Growing up, I hated my name. Bernadette is a big name for a small child. But even worse than my over-sized name is the inevitable shortened version. I was reminded of my distaste for the diminutive on two recent occasions, just days apart.

1. A charming young woman at a cocktail party told me she was a fan of *Daughter Lessons*. I was thrilled! Reading my blog, she said, made her feel like she knew me. So much so that she decided on the spot she was going to call me by the dreaded nickname. I hope I was polite, but more importantly, I hope I discouraged her.

2. A few days later, I met a new colleague who quickly declared I was so "cute" she just had to call me Bernie. Funny, upon hearing her proposal, I wasn't feeling cute. I was feeling more like the bear referenced in my name's meaning! Bernadette means "brave as a bear." Going forward, I will aim for more brave and less bear. Aside from those moments when I am "feeling the Bern," I actually think my given name suits me. Fittingly, there is a rose variety named Bernadette, but I have yet to find one named Bernie!

MY LITTLE TOWN

"Chase your dreams but always know
the road that'll lead you home again."
- Tim McGraw

I was born in Levittown, New Jersey, now known as Willingboro, but I don't consider myself a Jersey Girl. When I was three weeks old we moved to upstate New York, settling in Endicott. Like a lot of people, I have mixed emotions about the place I grew up because, by definition, growing up hurts and no one wants to be reminded of pain. Some of my biggest wounds were witnessed by my little town.

Grades 1-3: Picked last for gym, every week.

Grade 5: Father left; I told the nuns he was on a long vacation.

Grades 5 - 7: Walking to and from Grand Union several times a day, every day, with my Mom and little sister because we had no car but seven kids to feed. Our arms ached from the heavy bags.

High School: Pretending I was dumb or didn't care because smart kids were not popular. To make matters worse, pretending I was dumb didn't make me popular.

Grades 1-12: Mean girls. The names changed from grade to grade, but they were a common and constant theme. I was a mean girl magnet.

Ouch! Who would want to revisit the scene of those crimes? But as I drove there Saturday to take my mom to dinner, I recalled some of the good memories made in Endicott, New York:

- Pat Mitchell's ice cream. For $2, my mom and all 7 kids could get a cone of the most delicious ice cream known to man. Pat Mitchell himself told me every time he saw me I looked like Veronica Lake. I had no idea who that was, but it made me feel special.
- Meeting my first best friend, Andrea Schifano, when we were clouds in the 1st grade creation play at St. Ambrose.
- Andrea introducing me to Patty Toner — a dear friend to this day.
- Winning the Daughters of the American Revolution poetry contest and getting a congratulatory letter from the governor of New York (5th grade).
- Making the cheerleading squad in 9th grade (a coup for the girl always picked last for gym).
- Discovering in college that being smart was fun and being popular didn't matter.
- Club dancing every weekend with my steady college boyfriend and our pack of friends.

I also thought about the things that make Endicott great. Aside from the people that I love, most involve food: Spiedies, Duff's Pizza, Tony's, Nick's, Counsel's, Roma's Bakery, the free carousels, Enjoie Golf Course, Round Top Park and, of course, the Cider Mill.

I passed by the familiar red building with my mom and immediately recognized the smell of fall and some sweetness from my days in Endicott.

56

WRITE ON

"Knowing others is intelligence;
knowing yourself is true wisdom."
-Lao Tzu

I have been keeping a daily journal for more than a decade. I started at a very low point with the hope of writing through my challenges, but it has become so much more than that. Journaling has allowed me to know myself on the most essential level as I have asked and eventually answered the questions: Who am I? Where do I want to go? What do I need to get there? By answering those queries, I have co-created a beautiful life, although, when I started, I just wanted the pain to stop! Yes, I have come a long way since my first journal, where I was struggling to answer the simple question: What do you want? Eventually, I settled on a simple answer — a day without tears. But when my eyes finally dried, then what? That was when I started to design my future. I still use my writing time to dream and strategize how to make my dreams come true. The benefits of journaling are known and many, but I am often asked how to start. First, get a journal that will inspire you. You will look forward to filling it with your hopes, your thoughts, your desires. Find a place where you won't be disturbed. Use the timer on your phone to keep track of the precious minutes you are devoting to yourself. Start each session with a series of prompts that will help you gauge where you are mentally, spiritually, and emotionally (the answers will vary, daily).

My prompts:

- I am grateful:
- Special Prayers:
- Donations of the heart:
- Thoughts and ideas for a better tomorrow:
- Happiest Moment:
- What do I want:
- What I can count on today:

From there, I plot and plan; vent and venerate; design and dare. When you are down, words can help build you up. For example: write down five things you like about yourself. The best part of journaling is there are no rules. You can do with it whatever you want, however you want. Try it and discover the wisdom that comes with self-reflection. Famous people who have kept diaries/journals include: Leonardo DaVinci; Anne Frank; Harry S. Truman; C.S. Lewis; George Patton. A book to help you discover your authentic inner voice is *Writing Down Your Soul* by Janet Conner. Write on!

DO HAPPY

"Do things that make you happy
(within the confines of the legal system)."
- Ellen DeGeneres

The cover of my new journal, advising me to Do Happy, got me thinking. What makes me happy? That is a question many people, particularly women, fail to ask because we are wired to fulfill the needs and wants of others. Or sometimes we are merely going through the motions of what used to make us happy without evaluating if the thrill is still there. So, the first thing I wrote in my new journal was a list of simple things I could do any day, or every day, to experience joy. My list:

- dancing (impossible to be in a bad mood while dancing)
- music (all kinds)
- yoga (but NOT all kinds)
- reading (for pleasure)
- cleaning (yes, as in housework), and of course,
- writing (guess this means more blogs)!

Remember, how we spend our days is how we spend our lives, so make sure YOU do happy.

TALK TO STRANGERS

"Good things happen when you meet strangers."
- Yo-Yo Ma

Contrary to what your mother has said, you should talk to strangers. Common sense cautions apply, of course. But the next time you share space with someone you haven't met yet, consider putting down your device and starting a conversation. The results may surprise you.

I was on my fifth flight last week, seated with a man who looked as exhausted as I felt. I sized him up, concluding we had little in common. He looked to be in his 20s, not a business traveler, and when I heard him speak, it was obvious English was his second language. Despite our apparent differences, I dove in. In the span of a short flight, I learned that he was: 27 and in his final semester of a master's program; looking for work as a software engineer; from India but isn't sure it is "home;" being pressured by his parents to get married, though he has no girlfriend; and, in his opinion, is not good with women. He learned: My dad was a software engineer, and I am a lawyer; I have two daughters — neither in Rochester; I live there but am not necessarily staying; I am divorced and my family's reaction to it was worse than the break-up, itself; and, in my opinion, he only needs to be good with one woman, not womankind.

Appearances aside, software engineering and family issues closed gaps. As we continued talking, we discovered a deeper bond: we were both initiated into Kriya Yoga, a spiritual path followed by Mahatma Gandhi. Our conversation turned toward meditation and the quest for inner peace until we landed. As we exited the plane and I wished my nameless new friend a good life, I was so glad I talked to this stranger.

RESOLUTION REVOLUTION

"I hold it that a little rebellion, now
and then, is a good thing..."
-Thomas Jefferson

This year I am ready for real change. No more resolutions about losing 10 pounds or cleaning my closet. I want more for myself. Instead, I resolve to lose that which no longer serves me. I will cleanse the things that weigh me down or detract from that which brings me joy. This year I will live knowing I am more than my dress size, my bank account, my selfie. I will choose to have a happy heart, and not just on the weekend or when I am doing something fun. I will bring lightness to tasks that are burdensome, easing the strain for myself and those around me. I am going to sleep more, not to address the dark circles under my eyes, but so I can have more energy for things that actually matter. If per chance I am up all night, I will rejoice that I am living in a body that can take care of me even when I don't take care of it. I will stop the negative self-talk: I am so fat, I look so old, I am such an idiot, etc. Saying such things is hurtful to the one person who needs my love most — me. I will give myself a break, and by easing up on myself I will naturally be less critical of others. Each day will be an opportunity to live my resolutions. If I fall short, I will try again with the next sunrise. These goals are hard to measure. I won't be able to get on a scale to weigh success. These targets are reached moment by moment, measured by quiet satisfaction. Victory is attained each time I look past what's on the surface and see life's deeper miracles. And that is truly revolutionary.

HOLIDAY MANIFESTO

"Manifesto - a public declaration of intention,
opinion, objective or motive."
-Merriam-Webster Dictionary

Holiday is seldom paired with a manifesto. But I have been thinking a lot lately about how to spend the rest of my life, drafting statements about what I want and how I might achieve it. It is overwhelming. This morning, I concluded, it might be better to plan just for the next 30 days and see how I do. A month is less daunting, and my success (or failure) more readily measured.

This particular month (the one between Thanksgiving and Christmas) can be a source of great happiness or great angst. I decided to plan for the former and avoid the latter, at all costs.

My Holiday Manifesto: I will revel in this season. I will not complain about: snow, cold, traffic, or money. I will watch my favorite Christmas movie (*Holiday Inn*) more than once. I will take every opportunity to celebrate and decorate. I will drink champagne and eat Christmas cookies, maybe for breakfast. I won't stress about calories. I will wear sparkly shoes and a Santa hat at the very same time. I will spoil my children. I will sing Christmas carols at the top of my lungs. I will watch Courtney dance in the Nutcracker for the 16th year in a row. In the spirit of balance, I will be naughty and nice. If I have a bad moment, I will move on quickly. Yet I will positively linger under the mistletoe. I will offer those I love what they really want — my unadulterated presence. I will be the embodiment of joy! And perhaps if I manage to meet my 30-day plan, I will have the courage to tackle the next 30 years.

THE WAIT

"O come, o come Emanuel and ransom captive Israel."
-Traditional Christmas Hymn

I have been following a new ritual this advent. Every morning in December I have listened to a different version of the classic hymn "O Come, O Come Emanuel." There are many beautiful renditions (I like Casting Crowns and The Piano Guys best). For me, this song perfectly captures the longing common to each of us that walk the earth. When will our anticipation be fulfilled? That question has myriad answers — as many as the souls in wait. But before our yearning can be met, we must first realize that what truly satisfies doesn't come in a box or a bag, and likely is found not in the world, but inside ourselves.

CHRISTMAS PRESENCE

"Few delights can equal the presence
of one whom we utterly trust."
- George MacDonald

We all love to play Santa! But how do we balance making our daughters' (and sons') Christmas dreams come true with the message that Christmas is not about the presents? One of the beautiful women from Scott Miller Salon, Sara, asked me that question right before Thanksgiving. I immediately understood her fear about giving the wrong impression to her young children. I thought back to the days when my girls were small, knowing all too well the stress we place on ourselves to make the holiday perfect for our little ones. What I know now, as a more experienced mother, is that our children don't need perfection. They don't necessarily even want the things on their wish list. What they really long for is our time and our attention. If I could go back to those days, it wouldn't be to give my girls more things. It would be to enjoy their sweet presence and to let them enjoy mine.

WHAT REALLY MATTERS

"She who has not Christmas in her heart
will never find it under a tree."
- Roy L. Smith

It's December and expectation is in the air. Like most, my to do list is long and the available time to complete it is short. But this year, I am determined not to be pulled under by the tsunami of commercialism that attends the holidays. I look back on Christmases past and see how easily I fell into the trap of meeting superficial demands while failing to honor what I hold most dear. So, while I am thoroughly enjoying all the fun and frolic of a bedazzled New York City, each morning I am reflecting on what is truly sacred to me so I can be guided by my own ideals — not those offered by others. Consider: What is sacred to you, in your heart of hearts, and how can you honor it this season?

PASS THE POLITICS PLEASE

"Skip the religion and politics, head straight to
the compassion. Everything else is a distraction."
-Talib Kwell

As we pack up to go to our various Thanksgiving and Friendsgiving celebrations, I urge you to think twice before popping off over the popovers about politics, because no matter how ideologically in sync you believe you are with your peeps, you could be very wrong, and that is how arguments (and lengthy feuds) get started. Some become as stubborn as donkeys, while others develop memories for slights that would rival any elephant. Should the subject come up around your feast, don't take the bait. Change it to something safer. Like religion.

LOVE

MOTHERHOOD, PART I

"Romance fails us and so do friendships, but the relationship of parent and child, less noisy than all the others, remains..."
-Theodor Reik

This might be my favorite topic — of all time. I admit that there really isn't any lesson here, more like an essay on a subject that is very close to my heart. I love being a mother. It is the best, most fulfilling thing I have ever done, and I would start back at day one if I could and do it all over again. Not that I would have to, as I have no regrets. This doesn't mean that I think I have been a perfect mother. Both of my children could testify against me (under oath) that I have not been flawless or even close to it. I do believe that many would agree with me, however, that I love them perfectly and fiercely and endlessly.

When I was a little girl, I dreamed that I would have seven or eight children, probably because I came from such a gaggle of geese. I had some of their names picked out even: David, Dana (boy), Daryl (also a boy) Lee, Lynn. Unfortunately, that many children, unless you are married to a sheik, are not very practical or affordable. So, I apologize for not providing a wide variety of siblings. Besides, I think I would have been greatly overmatched! Final headcount aside, I knew from a very tender age that I wanted to be a mother.

We thought Carly was going to be a boy. Because Carly's Dad came from such a strong lineage of boys, we simply assumed that our first time out of the gate would produce a male. Also, I was "all baby" when I carried Carly and that made every person I ran into confirm our assessment.

Given her Dad's job, people were downright wishing that to be true under the premise that he deserved a male with whom to share his love of professional sports that are still largely dominated by males. Probably the best surprise of my life was in the delivery room when Dr. Peterson flipped Carly over and declared, "It's a girl!" This came on the heels of, "This baby is going to be a linebacker; I can barely get his shoulders out!" Rest assured, although thoroughly stunned, I was not disappointed. Carly was so beautiful — a perfect shock of dark hair, rosebud lips, and round, like a Botticelli angel. Pam, the labor and delivery nurse who was there when she finally appeared (after 17 hours of labor) said Carly was so pretty that she wanted to get pregnant again, and she did! When I returned fourteen months and one day later to have Courtney, she had just returned from maternity leave. Her third daughter arrived exactly nine months after Carly.

It is a little weird finally getting something that you have longed and waited for. I remember being stunned, really. I was tucked in the hospital bed, holding Carly, wondering "now what?" But those doubts melted away when a very ancient man and his equally ancient wife walked past our room. The door was wide open, and the man turned, holding onto his walker, to get a look inside. He then turned back to his wife with a smile and said, "Mother, look at this little girl and her baby. Isn't that great?" And it was — the beginning of something truly great.

MOTHERHOOD, PART II

"...the relationship of mother and child... indelible and indescribable... the strongest bond upon this earth."
- Theodor Reik

Please resist the urge to judge me harshly when I say, as soon as I had Carly, I could hardly wait to have another baby. I so enjoyed her and loved her so immensely, I wanted to give her a sister, or I assumed what would be a sister because I finally looked at the history of my family and realized that it didn't matter that Carly's Dad was one of so many boys, what probably mattered more was the fact that my Mom and my sisters had predominantly girls! But again, it really didn't matter. The real calculation was baby love + one more baby to love = great big giant love! That being said, I was not all that prepared to get pregnant when Carly was only five months old.

But pregnant I was and because I had just been pregnant the year before, I was accustomed to it. I must admit, I enjoyed my pregnancy with Courtney much more than I did with Carly. The reason for that is certainly because I knew the end game. I knew how wonderful it was to see someone come into the world and not just anyone, but someone whose existence depended on me and the man that I loved. That is pretty powerful stuff, and that knowledge helped me through pregnancy while working full time and adjusting to caring for a baby who was still well under a year.

Courtney arrived in mid-February, although she wasn't really scheduled to arrive until well into March. It was the coldest day ever. The wind chill was in the range of 50 below zero. Lucky for us, Court and I were safely inside Genesee Hospital; our only experience of the cold was everyone talking about it. It was also Chinese New Year 1991, which was very auspicious. Her arrival was memorable on many fronts.

The thing that I remember most is Carly's reaction to seeing Courtney for the very first time in the hospital. Carly arrived with her Grandmom and Grandpop only a couple of hours after Courtney had made her appearance. (She was so small, reminding me of a little bird. Especially in comparison to my then-recent experience of the robust baby Carly!) Grandmom put Carly in the bed next to me and she did not delay in trying to pull Courtney out of my arms! Poor Carly! She thought she had been replaced, which could never possibly happen; love + love was supposed to = more love!

I did worry about Carly adjusting to Courtney for the first six months or so. I felt so awful that my quest to add even more love to our little family might make her feel unloved or neglected. Well, it is a good thing that the end of this story is predictable. I knew everything was just fine and my plan had worked when I woke up one morning in August to find that Carly had climbed into the crib with Courtney (a sure sign of athletic prowess), the two of them laughing away. At that moment I knew I had given Carly one of the best things ever, a sister! My math equation was correct: love + love always equals even more love!

MOTHERHOOD:
A REALITY
SHOW

"Being a mother is learning about strengths you didn't know
you had and dealing with fears you didn't know existed."
- Linda Wooten

There is a disparity between what I dreamed of motherhood and
reality. That discrepancy has not produced disappointment. No,
the difference between the imagined and the lived has spawned
a profound respect for what all mothers encounter in the work of
raising children. Here is a look back on three unvarnished
moments from my own private motherhood.

Scene 1. Courtney was my shadow. No matter where we were,
she wanted to be next to me. When we went on play dates, the
other kids played; Courtney sat with me and the moms, drinking
coffee. I took her tendency to act like human velcro for granted
until the K-Mart incident. Courtney was five and intrigued by
Martha Stewart. She asked if she could go over to see the new
paint colors. This sounds precocious for a five-year-old, but she
was a born designer (she carried a Trading Spaces lunchbox for
years). I told her it was okay and watched her walk toward the
display, a mere 20 feet away. What I didn't realize was how busy

the store was and how small she was in contrast to everyone else in it. Before my eyes, she vanished. Panicked, I yelled her name. Nothing. I yelled again, loudly. No reply. I immediately began pushing through the bodies that had unknowingly come between me and my child, tears streaming down my face. When I finally reached her on the flip side of the display, she saw my crazed expression and started sobbing too. There we were in the middle of K-Mart, clinging to each other as if we had been apart for years, not seconds. But in those seconds, I had glimpsed a world without my precious girl, and it terrified me. Eventually, we learned to navigate being apart without that level of drama, but we have yet to return to K-Mart.

Scene 2. Seventh grade Carly begs me to go to a friend's house after school. I didn't feel good about it, but against my better judgment, I let her go. When I picked her up a few hours later, she is weirdly wearing a stocking cap that is completely covering her long golden hair. It is late April. I tell her to take it off. She refuses. I yank it off and discover her blonde hair is Ronald McDonald red! After the primal screams subsided, we tried to mend it ourselves. Be forewarned; bleach + red hair dye = pink hair. It was several days, boxes of hair dye and trips to the salon before golden locks were restored. In the long run, I learned to trust my inner voice and Carly learned only a licensed professional should dye her hair!

Scene 3. Carly is off to college. It is a milestone one looks forward to and dreads. I envisioned the tearful goodbye. Yes, all I had to do was play my part. Except — the big day did not unfold as planned.

Carly was bored and irritated with the setting-up process. Her father was just as irritated. If there was a dollar for every time he told her how grateful she should be for the chance to go to school in NYC, we would have had a good start on sophomore-year tuition. When it was time to say goodbye, they had had enough of each other, and I had enough of them. After searching my bag to give Carly cash before we left, I looked up to see the two of them hugging and weeping like babies. What? It was my chance to cry. This was my big moment of motherhood, only it wasn't because there they were carrying on...and on. Finally, it was too much. I turned to Carly and said with a big smile, "Get a hold of yourself; you are going to have the time of your life!" I then grabbed her weeping father and marched him away without looking back. I spoke to an ecstatic Carly, high on her newfound freedom, a couple of days later. She said, "Thank God someone was rational, Mom" when we discussed our abrupt departure. I realized by going off script, I gave my daughter permission to be happy — without me.

None of these moments are going to be featured on a Mothers' Day card (thank goodness), but these snapshots from my life — sans photoshop — are hallmarks of my motherhood.

LET'S DANCE

"And those who were seen dancing were thought to
be insane by those who could not hear the music."
-Friedrich Wilhelm Nietzsche

To me, dancing is one of the great joys in life. I have observed
that it is impossible to be in a bad mood when you are dancing.
Anyone who ever visited 70 East Blvd. knows that dancing is not
just part of our lives because Courtney happens to be a
professional dancer. Dancing is a part of our lives because we do
it spontaneously and often, and when we lived at 70 we danced
in every place imaginable but usually in the kitchen or in the
main hallway under the arch.

I would have loved to have learned how to dance like Courtney.
When I was a little girl, I wanted to take ballet lessons. The lack
of that opportunity was a function of both the lack of ballet
teachers in Endicott, New York and the lack of funds available to
Bernice Weaver (single mother) with her ever-hungry seven
children. My mom did buy me a pair of ballet slippers for my
birthday one year and I wore them gratefully. I knew even then
that having the right footwear is at least half of becoming what
you want to become.

I am happy to report that the lack of funds and ballet teachers did not prevent me from loving dance and from dancing, although my brand of dancing is nothing you would pay to watch.

Okay, let's just say it, I am more of a club dancer! And proud of it! I remember sneaking into a disco when I was a high school senior with my one-year-older friend, Cathy G. Most people snuck into clubs to drink, but we just wanted to dance. Once we were out there on the dance floor, we danced every single dance (the fast ones, anyway)! When I was finally "legal" and could get into clubs without a problem, we would go dancing every Thursday through Sunday night. I was a pretty cheap date because I spent most of the night on the dance floor and didn't really bother to have a drink until I got really thirsty from all that movement. When I was a senior in college, I did some local print and runway modeling (it was a small town, so the standards were not all that high). I remember one particular fashion show where everyone wanted to wear the waist length platinum blonde wig with a swath of heavy bangs in the front. There were at least 20 girls in the show, but they chose me to wear it in the finale because I was the best dancer! I was so excited, not so much about the wig (although that was cool) but because I had been declared the best dancer of the group! Validation is sweet.

PUPPY LOVE

"He is your friend, your partner, your defender,
your dog. You are his life, his love, his leader.
He will be yours, faithful and true, to the last beat of
his heart. You owe it to him to be worthy of such devotion."
-Unknown

Lessons from me wouldn't be complete without a chapter on Peanut. There is nothing in the world as wonderful as puppy love. The ironic thing is when this day started, I had a neighbor yelling at me about Peanut! Can you imagine? I had just finished taking Peanut for a morning walk. When we hit the top of our walkway, I always take him off the leash and watch him bound up the stairs to the front door. Watching his little legs climbing the stairs never ceases to amuse me. Today he spied one of the tenants from the apartment building next door heading for the bus stop just as I took him off the leash. Peanut ran in her direction and the woman freaked out. She was yelling at the top of her lungs, "I don't do dogs!" and "He better not touch me!" All the while, Peanut never got within two feet of her six-foot frame. Peanut simply stood there looking up at her, his tail wagging the whole time. The incident immediately turned me into a lioness protecting my cub. I scooped him up with one motion and carried him indignantly into the house. Doesn't she know, I said out loud, EVERYBODY loves Peanut?!

Peanut was my first official pet. Yes, dog walker was my first paid job, but I had to give those dogs back! I would never dream of giving Peanut back — ever. There are just so many good things about this dog. He loves fashion and looks good in all kinds of clothes. I think he may have been Marie Antoinette in a past life because I have never seen a living creature so comfortable with being dressed by someone else. When he was just a tiny puppy, I would come home from work and the girls would have him dressed up in American Girl Doll clothes. It was a hoot! My favorite was Felicity's granny cap and nightgown. Carly and Courtney would put him in the canopy bed on his back to play the part of the Big Bad Wolf to Felicity's Little Red Riding Hood. We have also had some great Halloween costumes for Peanut (superman, ninja, chicken, hot dog). Probably my favorite year was when Peanut and I were Paris Hilton and Tinkerbell, although we got the most mileage out of the cowboy costume, as Peanut was able to turn around and wear it to the academy awards the following February (the year of *Broke Back Mountain*).

Being fashionable has even come in handy for Peanut. One of my friend's huge German shepherds tried to pick Peanut up by the neck. If it weren't for the basketball jersey he was wearing, I shudder to think what would have happened. As it was, Peanut was dangling from giant jaws, his arms and legs moving as if he was running in mid-air. I yanked him out and ran for my life, trying to get away... all the while, Carly was laughing so hard she was on the ground.

Yes, Peanut is a fashion plate, it's true. But his best side is his inside — his soul. And Peanut has more soul than most. He is pure love and devotion, always happy to meet and greet whoever comes to the door or up the driveway. He loves all (including that mean Amazon lady who yelled at me this morning), and he loves me most of all, which is an honor. I am his raison d'être, and he is the only male in my life that has ever truly understood me. We are a match made in heaven and I am grateful for every minute I have with my true puppy love, Peanut.

MY THIRD CHILD

"If we learned to love the way our dogs love, the world would be a much better place."

-Book of Common Wisdom

I remember that night almost 16 years ago: the night before we got Peanut. I tossed and turned because I had no idea what I was going to do with the 18-ounce fur ball that was coming to live with us. I never had a pet before, but I had children. So, I decided I would care for Peanut like he was my child. And why not? The other two seemed to be coming along fine. Although a bookworm, I consulted not a single book. I conducted no research, despite my professional training. I made every call from my mother nature. When I realized Peanut wouldn't walk more than two houses before sitting down in protest, I bought an umbrella stroller and strapped him in so he wasn't left behind. I would rollerblade while pushing him along in a running carriage.

When he fussed, I scooped him up in my arms. Peanut weighed the same at full adult size that Carly weighed at birth (about nine pounds). He was my little guy and I was his Mama, one of the handful of words he recognized. If you asked, "Where's Mama?" he immediately looked my way. I protected and loved him with every ounce of maternal instinct I possessed. He, in turn, gave me his unabashed devotion. He stayed by my side through all the big upheavals: miscarriage, divorce, move, kids growing up and moving out. He was also there for the little moment: tending the garden, cleaning the house, writing (both briefs and blogs), my morning meditation. We traveled together by plane (Delta), train (NYC subway) and automobile (in his car seat). He ate what I ate and slept where I slept, most of the time. For the past few years, he came to the office with me nearly every day. Peanut was the silent witness to much of my adult life. While others may have questioned my decisions, he never once judged me harshly, or anybody else for that matter. Looking back, I can't remember a single person Peanut did not like. He was content with virtually anyone but preferred me above all, the highest of compliments. Last night again, I tossed and turned, struggling with the reality I was losing the only male who ever truly understood me: my third child. Today, though heartbroken, I am grateful I had the chance to receive such pure love and give it in return.

SMILE BECAUSE IT HAPPENED

"Don't cry because it's over; smile because it happened."
- Dr. Suess

It has been exactly one year since Peanut died. I am wistful at the thought of him. He was my constant companion, and I was the center of his universe. There was so much to admire about Peanut. He had a great walk, a strut really. He always attracted attention when we were out and about. He actually posed for the constant photographs we took of him and probably could have been America's top model, if he wanted to. But he would never need that kind of affirmation. He knew who he was and was satisfied just being with us. That was his job. He was the quiet (most of the time) guardian of our lives. He entertained and consoled us, cuddled and cheered us. Most of all, he reminded us of how lovable we are. With all that said, how can I remember him and do anything but smile?

MY GRANDMOTHERS

"We should all have one person who knows how to bless us despite the evidence. Grandmother was that person to me."
- Phyllis Theroux

My two grandmothers were completely different. Frances Kraszewski Augustine was only 18 years old when she had my mother on Thanksgiving Day in 1932. She was my young and glamorous grandmother. She always looked nice, her clothes were beautiful, and her hair, make-up, and nails were perfection. Even when she was in her 80s, she was stylish right down to her high heels, which she never gave up. She always giggled and laughed and seemed like a girl far more than she seemed like an adult, let alone a grandmother. She was the forerunner of today's shopaholics, hiding packages under the bed and behind the couch from my grandfather first, and then later on, Buss.

When she came to visit, it always felt like a vacation because she was a wonderful cook and baker. My mouth is watering just thinking of the food she made for us. She would make griddle cakes (which were like pancakes, only sweeter and more delicious), pot roast, the creamiest mashed potatoes imaginable, fruit cocktail cake, pineapple upside down cake, and lots of other sweets, which she loved most (she was very tiny but had an incredible sweet tooth).

Her best friend was her sister, Lenora, otherwise known as Shorty (who was even tinier). They married first cousins, Walter Augustine and Stanley Sherant. As adults, they lived just a couple of streets apart and the couples were often together, taking turns walking to each other's houses after dinner. She kept an immaculate home, one in which you really could eat off the floor. Although we spent many holidays at my grandmother's home on College Avenue in Elmira, I always associate her with Easter. We would have ham and other traditional Easter fare. I even remember my grandfather serving homemade strawberry wine. But the food that leaves the most lasting impression on my memory is the cupcakes we always had for dessert. They had pretty, swirled frosting and plastic Easter decorations stuck on top, like bunnies and ducks and painted eggs. I doubt I ate anything else on the menu; all I wanted were those cupcakes, which is why I make decorated cupcakes each Easter.

Because of my passion for cooking, cleaning, and homemaking in general, I am much like my mother's mother, which is why I am so proud I gave the eulogy at her funeral. Buss, her second husband of almost 20 years, asked me for a copy and told me later that he read it every day, making it one of the most important things I have ever composed. I have never written anything that meant so much to someone else. He told me that he fell in love with her the moment her saw her. She was in her early 60s and a widow after being married for more than 40 years. He was in his 70s. I am not sure where they connected, but I remember him saying that he never met anyone like her before in his life. They were really happy together and taught me that there is no age limit on love. As the years pass, you might be pleasantly surprised when love finds you long after its expected season.

Anna McDermott Weaver could not have been more of a contrast to her maternal counterpart. She was almost 20 years older than my mother's mother, giving birth to my father when she was 36 years old on June 26, 1932. She was decidedly not glamorous. She always wore her waist length black hair pulled back into a bun. She never used make-up, and she wore heavy shoes and stockings on her equally heavy legs. She did not go shopping for anything (my grandfather even bought the dresses she wore every single day) and only left the house to go to mass, and occasionally, to watch my dad at one of his sporting events. She was not a particularly good cook, and the only decent food I remember from the house at 202 Lake Avenue are molasses cookies (which were store bought). She drank tea with lots of milk from a white china cup with pink flowers. She loved to read and was always up on current events.

Probably the best thing about Grandma Weaver was her sweet little laugh — it remains in my ears to this day, despite the fact that she died just a couple of weeks after Courtney was born. Her laughter was often accompanied by the phrase "for pity's sake." She also had a wonderfully soft voice which ironically sounded exactly like Norine's (my dad's significant other). In fact, when I first met Norine, I was immediately struck by how much she sounded like my grandmother, especially when she would say my Dad's name in that drawn out melodic way of hers: "An than knee." I finally got the courage, after my Dad died, to ask Norine if he had ever mentioned that she sounded just like his mother. She said that he did and that he told her it was one of the reasons he loved her so much.

I loved to spend time with my Grandma Weaver. We would sit at her dining room table and go over her photo albums each visit. I never tired of hearing about my Dad's brother, Edward, a pilot whose plane crashed as he was returning home from World War II. Or about her mother, who died when she was only seven years old. She told me fun stories too. She grew up in the Germantown section of Philadelphia. Her father was a plumber, and everyone called him "Mac." She said that when the immigrants from Ireland arrived in Philadelphia, they were told, "Find Mac, and he will give you work." Grandma Weaver was one of nine children, but they were not poor — they had electricity, indoor plumbing, and all the modern conveniences. She told me all the men in the trades would help each other with their houses, so they had the best of everything. They even had a maid. The Philadelphia Federal Census record from 1900 shows my grandmother, age 4, listed with her parents (Thomas and Margaret) and her siblings, to date: William, Mary (May), Helen (who became a nun), Margaret, Alfonso (or Fonce) and Madeline.

Also listed with the family was Rosie Shields, occupation "servant." My grandmother used to tell me how they had Christmas trees with real candles on them. They would put the tree in the dining room and only light the candles when they ate, so they could make sure to watch for fires. She said they also had beautiful china dolls but were not allowed to play with them. For that purpose, they used rag dolls.

One of the stories that I loved best was how she took swimming lessons at the public swimming pool in Philadelphia when she was a single young woman in her early twenties. She paid for them with money she earned being a governess for the six children of a local doctor, Edward Moore. She said she was afraid to swim, so she set out to face her fears. I could not even imagine my ancient grandmother out of doors, let alone in a bathing suit. That story told me a lot about her and the kind of woman that she was. Whenever I am afraid, I think of her and try to face the issue head-on. I think of her fear and of her learning how to swim, anyway.

LUCKY GIRL

There are only two kinds of people in the world,
the Irish and those who wish they were.
- Irish Saying

It's St. Patrick's Day and while today everyone may be Irish, I am keenly aware not everyone is lucky enough to have an Irish grandmother. My Grandma Weaver was born Anna Kelly McDermott, and yes, she was 100% Irish. Anna Kelly McDermott was NOT a fiery Irishwoman; she was a gentle storyteller. I would listen to her talk for hours about growing up in a relatively wealthy family. But fortune turned at age seven when her mother died, leaving nine small children. The youngest, a baby, soon died too. Her father was so overwhelmed with grief, a contracting business, and his commitment to providing Irish immigrants with jobs, that he ultimately gave the children away. She lived with distant cousins until she was old enough to become a governess. She eventually married my grandfather, Frederick Weaver, a young widow with a young son. They raised eight children together during the toughest of times: The Depression, WW II, and the Cold War. They buried two of them. Despite her many heartaches, Grandma Weaver always had a twinkle in her eyes and a smile on her lips. I never heard her yell or complain. Her laugh was musical. My sister has a recording of her laugh which I have listened to many times, just to savor its sweetness. I think of her everyday — knowing I am a lucky girl to have had an Irish grandmother.

A NOT-SO-WICKED
KIND OF
STEPMOTHER

"Love comes from the most unexpected places."
- Barbara Streisand

At the risk of offending a host of people (except my subject), I must admit I adore my father's significant other. Although they were never married, I think of her as my stepmother. It was definitely not love at first sight, for me anyway. My tolerance for my father's ladies was typically low, and I had little hope Norine would be different from the others. The first time we met she had already moved in. She was obviously in love and surprisingly, he was too. Yuck. No matter how old, no child wants to see that. But then I noticed another change. Until then, there was no visible evidence in their home that my father had a single child, let alone seven, and upwards of a dozen grandchildren. Yet everywhere around us were pictures of my father's progeny.

As time went on, I discerned true tenderness between my hard-edged father and this humble woman. She was a teenaged mother and victim of domestic violence — ultimately fleeing her oppressor with five young children. She lost a second husband to cancer and her son was murdered (within months of each other). She and my dad met on New Year's Eve 1999 and never parted until he died, nine years later.

I still keep in touch with Norine, who is ever positive despite her many losses. We talk about how everyone is doing, and she always sweetly asks about my mother. But mostly she tells me things about my dad I never knew, and would never have known, but for her. I guess one never knows who will bear the greatest gifts.

FORGIVING OUR FATHERS

"Out beyond ideas of wrongdoing and rightdoing,
there is a field. I'll meet you there."
-Rumi

My father could best be described as difficult. Our relationship could equally be described as difficult. Consequently, I struggled each Father's Day, searching for the right card and inevitably concluding that the greeting card companies were woefully under-serving the market of children who did not have custodial dads. But like all children, I never gave up the hope that someday things would change. And they did — right in the nick of time.

When my father was dying, I had a vivid dream. He was lying in his hospital bed, enveloped by sadness. I watched myself approach and ask, "What's wrong, Dad?" He replied that he was sad because he failed me, had failed us, because he wasn't around. Without hesitation, my dream-self assured him, "Oh no, Dad. Don't you know, I picked you specifically? Everything I am and was meant to be unfolded perfectly, exactly as it is." Immediately, my father's face lit up like gold; he was at peace. I awoke, shaken but knowing this dream was important. A few days later, I wrote it all down and sent it to my father in a letter. He never mentioned receiving it, but six months later at his funeral, his significant other (Norine) told me that I had given him a tremendous gift. Ironically, I had given myself an even greater gift. I let myself see my dad for who he was, and who he wasn't, and chose to love him anyway.

I hope that you are all spending Father's Day with the dad of your dreams. Even if you are not, take a minute to be thankful and forgiving, no matter the circumstances. You will both be better for it.

LET'S PLAY BALL

"Never allow the fear of striking out keep
you from playing the game."
-Babe Ruth

If I could go back in time, I would find my father, but not as I last remember him, not even as the dad from my childhood. I would travel back, long before I was born, and watch him take the football field for Elmira Southside High School. This is an odd wish from a woman who was married to a sportscaster for 24 years, yet somehow managed not to take in a single sporting event. My dad made the city all-star team three years in a row, the last two for both the offensive and defensive teams. Football was not his only sport. He played basketball too, and baseball so well he was recruited by two major league teams. Although it would be wonderful to have a glimpse of his glory days, I was around for the most important of my dad's athletic career. I saw firsthand that, long after the victories of youth, he continued playing sports simply because he loved the game.

Sure, there were days when he still made headlines, like when he hit three home runs in three different games for three different teams on his 60th birthday! But the attention and awards never drove him. He was happy just to be participating and found a way to get out there, no matter what. After he was diagnosed with cancer at age 76, he insisted on finishing the season with his team. He would take his turn at bat and have someone else run for him. He never counted himself out, even if others might have. That last season revealed his champion spirit more than any other. Whenever I feel like I am too old, or too tired, or I am simply unmotivated, I think of my warrior father and say to myself, "Let's play ball!"

CARLY'S MOM

"All beings are beautiful seen through the eyes of love."
- Sai Baba

A piece of original artwork that Carly created for Mother's Day when she was in first grade may be my most prized possession. It hung proudly in the main hall of 70 East Blvd. and will grace the walls of any and all of my future homes. When visitors comment about it, I cannot help but utter, "It looks just like a Modigliani."

I know the piece is not the most accurate depiction of me. The lashes are thicker, darker, and longer than mine. The face is a perfect oval with a much more distinguished nose. The lips she fashioned would be the envy of any woman — a full heart-shaped red bow! I have not, and will never again, look quite so good.

No, my daughter's enhanced perception does not disappoint. And although her lens of adoration may have resulted in a somewhat misleadingly lovely portrait, I note that Carly was quite astute in capturing the proud gaze of a young mother who was quite pleased with her precious girls.

May the eyes of true love shine on each of you, today and always.

DON'T FORGET THAT SPECIAL SOMEONE

"To love oneself is the beginning of a life-long romance."
- Oscar Wilde

It's that day again! The day dedicated to celebrating love. I was picking up some last-minute Valentines when a coffee mug captioned "I love me" caught my eye. Although it was meant as a joke, it actually is the key to it all. Sure, it has been said before, you have to love yourself before you can truly love anyone else, but those words are worth repeating. For many, self-love is their biggest challenge. So, while you are expressing your affection for those you adore on this day of love, don't forget where it all begins. Go to yoga, watch your favorite romantic film, curl up for a half hour with a book or magazine — do something for yourself, and celebrate the love of your life!

THE GREATEST GIFTS

"The most important thing that parents can teach
their children is how to get along without them."
- Frank A. Clark

My dad was blessed with the genetic trifecta: he was smart, athletic, and movie-star handsome. You may think that affection affects my accuracy, but I have the photos, awards, and eyewitness accounts to prove it! Funny thing, those attributes never enter my assessment of him. By the time I arrived, child six of seven, my dad's good looks and hair were both running thin. I was only aware of his sports prowess because I was dragged to boring softball games. And when he tried to explain his work in computer programming, he may as well have been speaking Fortran.

I adored my dad because he sang me to sleep when I was afraid. He never told me I was pretty; he always told me I was smart. He armed me with the power of multiplication (to 12), turning punch cards into flashcards and drilling me until I had them down cold. He showed me how to use a hammer and nails, as well as the critical difference between a Phillips and a flat head screw. The phrase right tight, left loose will forever be embedded in my brain. His deep bass voice and 8-track tapes introduced me to Nat King Cole, Dionne Warwick, and the musical Camelot (I know every song by heart). He gave me countless examples of how to stand up for myself. And in the end, he taught me about humility, accepting the ravages of disease and impending death while coming to terms with a life he felt was unfinished. Some gifts are obvious to the world, but some are only discernible to the eyes of a child. And those are the greatest gifts of all.

DAUGHTERS NEED DADS

"A daughter needs a dad to be the standard
against which she will judge all men."
-Anonymous

Dads have been on my mind lately. Sunday was Father's Day and yesterday would have been my dad's 83rd birthday. I thought of him quite often this week, and most weeks. I find this somewhat ironic in that I lived much of my life without my father. He left our home when I was 10 and for many years, I rarely saw him outside of strained dinners with me and my little sister, meals that lasted barely an hour because he had to go back to work. I don't think I realized the size of my loss until I had my own daughters. They have a father who would sooner dive into a tank of sharks than not be part of their daily lives, even now that they are grown and living in other cities. Seeing my daughters' solid relationship with their dad has helped me acknowledge the part of me that was compromised by largely growing up without mine. Cheryl Strayed says it best: "The father's job is to teach his children to be warriors, to give them the confidence to get on the horse to ride into battle when it's necessary to do so. If you don't get that from your father, you have to teach yourself." Eventually, I learned how to confront my enemies; part of that fierceness was in me all along. A. A. Weaver was a formidable, fiery man. When I need to be strong or forceful, I channel him. I only wish I had seen him in action more often. Anyone who reads my blog knows I love my mother and my motherhood, but this week I thought it was time to give a shout out to the fathers. We need you too! Anyone who has doubts about the importance of dads, read Meg Meeker's *Strong Fathers, Strong Daughters*. I have recommended that book to every man in my life that has a daughter. Love to all dads... and their daughters.

WHY LOVE WINS

"Love conquers all things; let us, too, surrender to love."
-Virgil

The Supreme Court legalized same-sex marriage last week. It was exciting to see the wave of Instagram photos proclaiming, simply, Love Wins! As a lawyer, I knew it was not that simple, so I had Jayne print the 100+ page decision and dissents so I could learn more. Below is a quick synopsis so that you too will know not only that Love Wins, but why.

The name of the decision, written by Justice Anthony Kennedy, is *Obergefell v. Hodges,* and in it the Court considered: 1. the constitutionality of state bans on same-sex marriages, and 2. whether states had to recognize lawful same-sex marriages performed outside the state. The Court decided that under the 14th Amendment, the bans were unconstitutional and states must recognize lawful same-sex marriages. The Court declared the right to marry "fundamental" to a person's liberty and that right and that liberty are guaranteed by due process and equal protection. The decision is quite eloquent. I urge you to read it for yourself (the syllabus/summary is 5 pages; the decision, 28). The main thrust of the dissenting opinions (judges who voted against) is that this issue should be decided by voters — not the

Court — and that the states should be able to have their own rules.

So, after satisfying my lawyer self, I couldn't help but marvel at the progress we have made, as a society, in a relatively short period of time.

Only a century ago, it was unlikely that people of differing social classes would marry. The union of people practicing different religions was also taboo. Less than 50 years ago, it was illegal in some states for people of different races to marry — an injustice ultimately addressed by the Supreme Court in *Loving v. Virginia* (1967). And now another barrier to love has fallen! As I often do when I am pondering life, I consulted my personal source of wisdom, my mother. Bernice Weaver has seen a lot of changes in her more than 80 years. Given her strict adherence to Catholicism, I was not sure what she would say, but she did not disappoint. When I asked her what she thought about the legalization of gay marriage, she admitted it was a big change. "I don't know, Bern" was her initial response. But in the end, she sweetly and perfectly summed it up: "I guess everyone deserves to be happy, so it's a good thing." Amen! Awomen!

WHY I ADORE MY MOTHER

"All that I am or hope to be, I owe to my angel mother."
- Abraham Lincoln

My mother holds a wine glass like the Statue of Liberty holds her torch. She can wear a holiday sweater and look perfectly hip. She gives great advice without being preachy or condescending. My mother appreciates even the most modest of offerings and will praise the giver to the point of embarrassment! She may not agree with you, but she will always take your part. My mother has seen it all at least once, but still manages to look at life with new eyes. Last May, she was the flower girl in my nephew's wedding — she said it was the happiest day of her life! She is skilled at buying lotto tickets and knows how to ask for all the different ticket combinations. She is afraid to use my coffee maker and of my seven-pound dog, but unafraid of teenagers, divorce, sickness, or death. My mother has her own language. Oprah Winfrey is "Ofrah Wimprey" and Geraldo Rivera is "Rennaulto." They are fancy TV stars who ride in "lemozines." More importantly, she speaks the language of prayer, dedicating each day to a particular family member. There are so many of us, she is on a schedule! But she is never too busy to pray for anyone who asks. She is kind, she is classy, and she is fun! I adore my mother for all these reasons and many more, but most of all because she is pure love. Mamaste!

SWEET GOODBYES

"How lucky I am to have something that
makes saying goodbye so hard."
-Winnie the Pooh

Courtney left today and won't be home again until Christmas. We had such fun during her "off season" from the Dayton Ballet. But it went way too fast, like all the time I spend with my girls. Perhaps the hardest part of being a parent is being separated from your children as they grow up, and often, away. Thank God for the modern conveniences of cell phones, texting and Skype — they really do make it easier to stay in touch. But technology cannot replace being with someone in person. There is something sacred in sharing space, breathing the same air, just being together. It was with great joy that I discovered Courtney left her favorite water bottle and had to return for it before hitting the road with her dad. At least when she left the second time, I remembered to grab a picture of her and Peanut sharing one final snuggle. No, goodbyes are never easy, but they are sweet when we know that we send our children out into the world, armed with love and our faith in them.

POSTSCRIPT

Little did we know that we had another farewell in our future. On Sunday afternoon, our 100-year-old apple tree collapsed under the weight of a bumper crop of apples! I was in Buffalo for the evening and received a kind phone call from our neighbor, Sandra, who wanted to warn me before I unknowingly happened upon the tragic scene. Oh, what sadness!

We, including our many friends and neighbors, loved that tree. She was the quintessential survivor. Though a cement block ran through her trunk to keep her standing, she bloomed magnificently in the spring and gave us crisp apples in the fall. I was comforted I took a final picture and amazed at how prophetic the title Sweet Goodbyes really was. I have been saying goodbye (yes, I hugged her several times) and eating apples all week. We are grateful for the years she graced us and are looking on the bright side as much as we can. We have a better view of the sky and the garden now. I am reminded of a favorite quote, which comes in handy at times like these: "The barn burned down; now I can see the moon."

Made in the USA
Middletown, DE
03 September 2023

37642550R00070